HEATHER ROBINSON'S SELECTED WORKS

I0223696

INCLUDING

TRANSLATIONS AND SILENT VOICES

chipmunkapublishing
the mental health publisher

Heather Robinson

Published by
Chipmunkapublishing
PO Box 6872
Brentwood
Essex CM13 1ZT
United Kingdom

http://www.chipmunkapublishing.com

Edited by Heena Kausar

Chipmunkapublishing gratefully acknowledge the
support of Arts Council England.

SILENT VOICE AND TRANSLATIONS

Sat there, looking out of the window, silent. Her eyes were sore, but now dead and emotionless from days of crying. She now had what she wanted, but didn't know whether it had been the right decision. Anyway, there was no going back now.

The past six months had been hell for Helen. Now sixteen, just, she had only been clubbing with her girlfriends the week before. Now here she was in a secure room, being watched in an adolescent mental health unit.

Her dad had just visited, but she had asked him to leave when becoming too hysterical to hold a conversation. She wasn't afraid, wasn't in danger by the people she was now controlled and monitored by, but refused to admit to herself that someone else could tell her things about her own mind that she couldn't understand or work out for herself.

It had started as long ago as she could remember; Seven years old and a very happy, popular child. Her eyes as deep blue as her fathers and long dark hair just like her mother.

She remembered with flashbacks how the nanny that looked after her and her brother threw her across the room with frustration. Her head flinched as she remembered hitting the floor. She never shared this with anyone as when she attempted to try, she saw no way that the six foot woman who was in charge of her childcare could not somehow manipulate her accusations to her favour.

In giving up on trust, she started counting anything and everything. Daring herself to steal and swear when no one could hear, it was a way of keeping some form of control, some sort of secret between her and her own mind. However, now it was her own mind that had turned against her and trust was necessary in her recovery.

The weight loss didn't happen until a year ago. Having learnt to control the counting and routines, she went to secondary school again, a very popular and happy teenager.

"Be careful how high you climb, as the fall is a lot further and faster at the top."
The words of her head of year, Mr Monty now rung in her ears making sense for the first time.

The past four years had been a walk in the park. Girls nights out, no serious exams yet, testing everything that life threw her way, like any other hedonistic teen.

She had managed to put behind her that fateful night when, at eleven years old, her cousin had managed to get his way with her in bed. She vowed to herself then that sex would never be on the agenda before marriage, and men would never be allowed to take advantage again.

Having stayed true to this, just before her sixteenth birthday, the testing time would come again. Most of her friends had long since lost their virginity having hung round with the older lads in town for a while.

Not Helen though, "if I sleep with you, you will soon forget about me and lose all your respect. We would not be having this conversation if I had have slept with you." That is what she said to the lad she had been seeing ever since the topic cropped up.

Tonight was slightly different though.

"I've got to meet my dad now outside the cinema; he'll go mad if I'm late." Said Lou.

"Hang on a sec', I thought you said I could stay at yours" Helen said.

"Oh, shit yeh, sorry he won't let you, he's being funny again."

"Oh great, so what the hell am I supposed to do now?" Helen panicked.

"Why don't you sleep at Brian's'?" was the inevitable reply

That was the first problem. Now after midnight, it was far too late to get a bus home or get picked up as she lived six miles out of town. She either slept at her boyfriends or on the streets. They had all been drinking all night, later on Brian slipped something into her vodka and lemonade.
"What was that?" she asked

"Well, it's not Panadol" laughed Brian's' mate Adam.

She was far gone by now and didn't really care what was in it anyway as she assumed that Lou had set her up anyway and didn't believe for one minute that she had ever asked her dad.

Later that night, Brian took her back to the house he shared with his mum and aunt, still being a student. As he led her upstairs, she knew what was coming but thought that he would just accept foreplay. This obviously did not happen and after an hour, in agony she asked that it stopped. It didn't and it was three hours later before this 'one-way' pleasure fest ended.

The next morning she woke, ashamed, scared and numb. Brian was in the shower so she looked round the room or her phone. As she picked it up from the table by the window, she noticed a letter with kisses all over it.
Looking around to check Brian was out of the way, she opened it and read. A great lump appeared in her throat and stomach as she read the three pages of loving verse from Brian's long term girlfriend. Having no idea of this relationship, she quickly put it back and got dressed.

She phoned Jo to see if she could come round, but apparently it was 'family day' and there was no chance. "Funny" she thought, "it's different when you need a friend". Only last week Jo had described her as a sister.

So, she didn't dare go home due to the shame, her other friends were all at work or having 'family days' so she sat on a bench by the bank in town; Staring into space, eyes sore and numb, and the rain not being a distraction. She had now lost her appetite completely and noticed that she hadn't had her period this morning. Despite having just lost three stone in weight in the past three months, instead, she put this down to the possibility of being pregnant as the condom split the night before.

As she looked out of the window, she was brought back with flash by the student nurse, Denise.

"What is it you are afraid of?" she asked.

"I am not afraid of putting on weight. It's the not wanting to that scares me. Do you know what I mean?" she replied.
This was to be the sentence that defined the next six years of her life, but no matter how hard she tried, she didn't think anyone could possibly understand.

"Hey how are you? I'm Sarah"
"I'm Christine"
"I'm Nicky"

The other girls in the clinic had grabbed a chance at introductions when the nurse went downstairs for 'handover'.

"Hi I'm Helen, sorry, I'm not gonna be much fun today, I just got here. I think I made a mistake, there doesn't seem to be much group therapy or treatment does there?" Helen asked.

"Ha, no there's only food in here as any medication. We talk to key workers and stuff but they just give you books to read." said Sarah.

"We're always here to talk to though, you know. There's Phil, he's sixteen as well. He's schizophrenic. Then there's Mandy, she's manic depressive, and little Kat, she's the same as us but she's only twelve bless her." she continued.

"Yeh," added Christine, there's new people coming in on Thursdays as well. Who have you got?"

"She means who is your key worker" explained Sarah.
"Oh! Anna." Helen answered.

"Oh that's ok, she's alright. Just as long as you didn't get Rachael, she's a right gobshite. She's on leave thought at the moment as she was running after Mandy last week and broke her ankle in a rabbit hole." Sarah laughed. The other girls enjoyed remembering it for a second, before being called away by the duty nurse.

"See you when you're allowed down then" Christine shouted.
"Yeh, see you." Helen answered.

God, she couldn't believe this situation. Last Friday she had been clubbing in town with friends, trying to forget her GCSE's. Now, she was living in hospital amongst the insane! It was like stepping into a TV screen or researching a thriller.

For the next few weeks, once she was allowed off suicide watch she roamed around with the other girls.

"Wanna come for a walk to get those calories burning away?" asked Christine.
"Er, yeh sure, hang on a sec', I'll get my jacket".

They were allowed levels of monitoring once the weight progressed, and by now Helen was on level 3 which meant that in between meals she could pretty much go wherever she pleased.

What Christine had said, though had struck a chord in Helen, as her worst fear once the treatment had started was that she would still WANT to lose weight. This was obviously apparent in the other girls and she came to the stage of thinking that if she couldn't beat this illness, why not just join in with the others.

This would be a good attitude in a sport or study group, but it was the decision that potentially ruined the next six years of her life.
She soon started hiding food, dancing in her room, ran around the fields behind the unit, drank water before 'weigh day', and learnt every trick in the book that she had never even considered before.

One week later, her exercise had been noted by the nurses. Her key worker had been away studying since her admission to the clinic, so it was the other staff that controlled her levels. She had just been told that she would not be allowed out anymore until her weight went up, not down.

So, again, staring out of the window, she started thinking again. This led her into a daydream of her grandmother's burial.

After the nanny had been fired, through smashing her bedroom door made from reinforced glass, it had been her grandmothers that took over the babysitting. They moved in and became like a second set of parents for her and her brother. They gave her first cigarette, loved being around her friends, and loved her for the shopping she did and general companionship.

When she was fifteen, studying for her mock exams, her grandma had wanted to live independently. As she wished, the family found her some safe accommodation in the next village. She had been taken to hospital after an apparent fall, but on going to the flat, Helens father had found blood and excrement stained walls, furniture and carpets. They had hidden the details from her mother, but Helen had never understood what kind of illness could cause such a death.

She remembered when her father had removed the casket from the graveyard at night. It stayed in the boot of the car until the day she went with her mum to the graveyard that she wanted to be scattered over.

She could still smell the stale smell and began to feel sick, remembering. It was raining and took nearly half an hour to find her grandmothers parents gravestone. Eventually, she spared her mother the trauma and opened the wooden box.

Unlike what you see in films, there was no charcoal, light flakes of ash. Instead, a bin bag filled with hardened, bone meal like white remains of her best friend's bones. She pulled bits of, piece by piece and the rain made it stick to her face.

"Helen, Helen! Are you coming down for your drink?" asked Jill, the nurse.
"Helen, now please." She ordered.
"Don't these people have any heart, any feelings?" She thought.
The cruel undertones were to get worse that night.

Christine, who had not found it as easy as everyone else to come to terms with the tactics of the clinic was struggling at supper. Using every distraction as possible, it was like pulling teeth.

"Don't worry." Helen mimed to her, gently.
"Oh for God's sake! I'm sick of working with such selfish, self-obsessed girls. You could all do with going onto a normal ward and seeing what REAL illnesses are all about!" Wendy the nurse shouted in fury.

With that, every one by one walked out of the room and went upstairs. There was nothing she could do as she was outnumbered, but this was the deciding factor for Helen, that if nurses really felt this way, there was no hope of coming out of here with anything having changed in her mindset.
She knew that to the outside world, she was scum on the ground, but expected the staff to understand, at least.

For her, the 'therapy' was now well and truly over, as it was with the other girls. Instead, she spent the last couple of weeks of her time there, rebelling; Setting off the fire alarms, getting drunk by the tree in the back garden, smoking too much, and planning an escape with her new 'partner in crime,' Jasmine. Jasmine had been admitted after attempting suicide. She was not at a low weight, and seemed to suffer no mental illness, but had to be kept there as a precaution.

Helen got on with her because she found it refreshing to be with someone with no label. She had never assumed herself Anorexic in the first place, as she never actually starved herself, and didn't think she was fat. No, Helen just ran and ran and ran, to sort of relieve her of all the thoughts that she couldn't escape about her grandma, exams, sex and a very distressing bike accident, in which she couldn't recognise herself after her face took full impact of the tarmac.

SILENT VOICE AND TRANSLATIONS

One day, she was called in for a consultation. This was the first time she had seen an ACTUAL psychologist since her arrival.

"Hello Helen, my name is Gary White, I'm the consultant clinical psychologist, do you mind if we have a chat for a while?" he asked.

By now, Helen was sick of being spoken to like a dependant, demented little girl, and it showed on her face.

"Do you know about the war theory?" the Doctor asked.
"No" she answered bluntly.

"Right, well there was once a comparison made to men that were starved during the war. It was found that the lower in weight they got, the more pre-occupied with their body image they became." He explained.

"Yeh, that's great, but if it's true, how do you explain the fact that I have been putting on weight for a month now and I do not feel any better than when I first came here." She said.

"Well, let's see shall we." He answered.

He then left, which puzzled her. This was the top guy in here, she thought. If that is all that comes from being trained as a doctor, what chance has anyone got at recovery from this? "This is just bullshit" she thought.

Beginning by now to feel like a factory-reared chicken, she was finally glad when discharge day finally arrived. It didn't really go as planned, or expected. Most of the other girls had left now, so it wasn't fun anymore. Desperate to get home and go back to work, and indeed go running again, she had no problem expressing this when she found out that morning that her weight was the minimum required for release.

She was asked just one question, to her surprise by the consultant.
"Do you have any suicidal thoughts?" he asked.
"No." she answered.
Why would she, she thought. She didn't want to die, that would take away the ecstatic feelings of achievement at losing all the weight again.

The inevitable did happen, but not without a fight. The family were well know due to owning the hotel, so the locals that knew of the problems all put in there ten penny worth of advice.

In a desperate attempt, Helens mother called in a spiritual healer.
"Lie down on your back and close your eyes." the 'healer' said.
The woman started manoeuvring her hands across Helens stomach, while chanting.

"Ahhh, uuummmmm, aaaahhhhhrrrrggghhhhh...."
She shrieked.

Helen sat up straight, wondering what on earth was going on.

"It's ok; I've just removed the negative energy from your body." The healer said.

Next, she tried hypnotherapy. After fours hours lying down, Helen lost hope of relaxing into a coma and just went along with what was asked.

"Think of a colour." He asked.
"Green";

"Ok, now think of an animal."
"A rabbit."

"Right, every time you get these thoughts, give them to the green rabbit and he will carry them away." He said.
"What?" she thought. "He's madder than me!"

Finally, Helen and her mother went to see a clairvoyant who had advertised herself as a having worked with celebrities in rehab.

They went to a private, rather posh office in the city centre.

"Watch your back, I can see a man in uniform, and your problems have been caused by the meddling in black magic at some stage. Is this true?" the clairvoyant asked.

Helen looked at her mother, trying not to laugh, as she remembered clearly doing ouija boards and séances in the hay barn with her school mates, but she wasn't exactly a witch.

The end of this madness came when she went to see a private psycho-therapist; Psycho being the main word.

After having sat through hours of sessions, she was once again, post gym work-out sat in the chair of his house. There had been many sessions where she doubted his professionalism. He suggested that she slept with as many men and women as possible to determine her sexuality, despite knowing of her past relationships. He told her that if she didn't drink at college, she would never fit in, despite him knowing about her incontrollable drinking at school and experimenting in soft drugs. He also suggested that she join the army, as he had done to satisfy her need for exercise. Surely though, this was what she came to him for help about, not encouragement.

"So you are telling me that your health is not important to you?" Tim asked.
"No, I'm not saying that, you don't understand." She answered.
He then lunged forwards with his fist clenched up to her face and approached her closely.

"Don't understand, don't understand! My brother died from pneumonia caused by bulimia, don't you ever tell me that I don't understand." He shouted.

SILENT VOICE AND TRANSLATIONS

Now petrified, she quickly ended the session and phoned for a lift home. It was clear that people saw her as evil, rather than the state of mind she was in. She wrote him a long letter on how he shouldn't be working in mental health, as he was too personally connected with the illness.

By this time, everyone had just got back into their own lives, and given up on any full recovery. It was up to Helen now, as she was past the age of being able to be hospitalised without her own permission, or a section, which her family would never consider.

Two years later, after having worked in the family hotel that had just gone bankrupt, she was headed for college in the next major city. She was unsure; as it was the first time she would be going back to that town since the time on the ward. She thought that she could avoid that part of the city though. She moved into a renovated stable block just up the road from the college, sharing with loads of other students.

She had chosen childcare as a two year course and had focus; to begin with.
Having no GCSE's due to her time in hospital, she got in on her mock exam results which were very impressive. Her past condition also helped convince the tutors that she wanted to sort her life out.
"Hey you come out tonight? I know it's your first night and everything but we wanna show you around before college starts." Asked Liz her flatmate.

"Er, yeh why not." She agreed.

They went to a local club in the city, and despite looking around cautiously for nurses; Helen managed to have a good night.

"You know, Helen, I think you're goon a fit in just fine. You're a right laugh, mate." Liz said.

Helen went to bed that night a bit confused. She was on a good course, made good friends, lived in a nice area, but this sense of security felt somehow wrong. She started to feel guilty at being happy again; it felt uncomfortable, selfish even.

The next three couple of weeks went ok. The problems began when she started getting despondent about the course. It was 99% political, and having worked for a nursery, she didn't feel that this was the 'childcare' she had signed up for. The content was all about what you couldn't do with children, not about what she enjoyed most which was the interaction with the kids.

Having slept in one day after a particularly late night out, she went downstairs and started to pick at a sandwich. Feeling bored, she started to feel hot and bit at her nails. This panicky state of mind was all too familiar and it only took ten minutes to decide to cycle home; All twenty five miles home.

As she felt the wind on her face, she felt less and less stressed. That night, she cycled back again before dark. One other girl cycled everywhere as well so at first people didn't find it particularly extreme.

"Your arms are so skinny, mate." Holly announced.

SILENT VOICE AND TRANSLATIONS

"Yeh, I'll grow in time! 2 Helen tried to joke."
She went to bed that night thinking that people were becoming suspicious. Two weeks later, she had quit college and was back at home, one stone lighter.

"I've got a new job" Helen announced.
"Where is it?" asked her mother.

"Well, it's in Shrewsbury, but it's really good, I'm working for a children's holiday camp training as an activity instructor."

"Do you not think that you should try and get a bit better before going?" said her mother, being careful of the eggshells.

"Look, this might make me better won't it? I won't be able to eat too little in front of all those people will I? I mean, I'm sharing a campsite with about three hundred staff!" She answered, slightly unconvinced.

The training course was ten days long and it was relatively easy to cover up her arms, until she was given the uniform, a t-shirt. The summer was proving a blisteringly hot one and it was impossible to cover up.

"So how did you get into sports then?" Helen asked Jane, a fellow trainee sharing the tent.

"I've always gone walking, but just wanted to get out of London. I've done all the peaks." She said.

"Really, I've done one of them, but would love to go up to Scotland." She answered.

"You know, you have to be fit to go hiking, don't you?" noted Jane.
At this came no reply, as Helen could sense that the tone had changed.

"Helen, can we have a word with you?" asked Dawn, the other girl sharing the tent.

Helen knew what was coming and prepared her defence.
"You know that you can talk to us whenever you want don't you."
"What do you mean?" Helen asked."
"Well, I'm studying psychology at Surrey University next year, and, well, we noticed the bag under your bed." Dawn continued.
"For God sake, look, my weight has always been low, and my mother sends build up drinks and protein bars in the hope that I have enough with me; I 'm not bulimic if that's what you think." Helen answered firmly.

This was true, though, as Helen had Salmonella as a child and had always had a phobia of sickness. It was a tough one though. If she bought a cake in the supermarket, people assumed she was throwing up, if she bought a lettuce and diet coke, people assumed she was starving.

Later that day, Dawn cornered her.

SILENT VOICE AND TRANSLATIONS

"Look, Helen, I want to be a nurse because I used to have a problem. I know what it's like. I'm worried that you could have a heart attack or something on this course, so maybe you want to consider telling the training staff."

"Hey, I'm sorry about your past, but I don't have a problem and I'm not leaving." She answered.

"Fine, it's your decision, but if I think you could be in danger, I will tell them myself." Dawn ended.

Oh great, Helen thought. Tell them what exactly? She knew that she had no option but to leave now though, as she couldn't imagine sharing a tent and her life, with another trainee psychologist or nurse after what had happened in the clinic.

"Yes, ok if you think that your appendix operation was too recent to continue working with us then we'll arrange transport for you back to the train station at the weekend. You'll have to earn your board though by helping the cleaning staff and general work around the site." Her boss said.

She didn't know whether they were doing it on purpose, but since the day that she ran back through the woods, to escape the absailing that would leave her emaciated arms open to public view, Helen had worked harder than she had on the course. Every two seconds, "Helen, run back to the office and get my file" or "Helen, all the beds need doing before lunch".

What was now frightening was that she could no longer control her weight. For the first time in her life she was actually worried about her health. No matter how much she ate, it went straight through her and she literally couldn't stop losing weight. Her body had decided it had had enough, and the train did not stop at home as planned.

Instead, In order to avoid the lecture at home, she went to stay with her best friend, Emily and her fiancé, Jason in Wales.

She had not planned to stay there long, but Emily worked at a café in the town during her stay, so she soon found herself looking for work. Instead of taking the bus, she sometimes walked the ten mile journey into town. Old habits die hard, or not.

Having worked a shift at a B&B in the next village, she realised that she missed home. North Wales was quite desolate unless you were on holiday, or were Welsh, she thought.
The journey back seemed to fly by as she tried to figure out how she was going to be acknowledged at home.

"I'm at the train station, can you pick me up?" she asked, wearily.
"I suppose I'll have to, won't I" was the answer from her father.
She thought that if she was going to stay home for good, she would have to learn to drive, quickly.

SILENT VOICE AND TRANSLATIONS

A couple of weeks later, she was back in the same old routine of finding work, walking and trying to piece together her social life. Her image now though had turned into 'the girl that's ill' no matter how hard she worked, or how out-going she tried to appear.

"I'm only paying for your driving lessons if you keep at it until you pass, not like everything else you give up." said her mother.

"Look, I never asked you to pay for anything, I'll walk and take the bus to work, it doesn't bother me" was the reply.

Her mother knew this all too well though. Helen would practically walk all the way into town and back if she had to. Her worry was that her temper could be so volatile that she didn't know whether her learning to drive would prove even more fatal.

It was nearly Helens' twenty first birthday and she was aware of the preparations.

"How can I possibly face a surprise party with all my friends and family when all I have physically achieved in twenty one years is mental illness." she thought.
This was not entirely true, as she had experienced more than the average person at middle age by the time she was eighteen, but she only ever reflected on the negatives.

"Mum, I've got a job in Barnsley. I go tomorrow."
She announced.
"What! But, you can't, you can't, it's your birthday in
two weeks." Her mum shouted.
"Look, it doesn't matter about my birthday; it's just
another year, right." She replied.

Her mother looked on, as she got in the taxi to the
station. There was nothing she could do. She didn't
know whether Helen had found out about the party
but she would know have to phone everyone and
cancel. This was the desired outcome for Helen, as
she didn't want her parent's spending money on a
party that would prove embarrassing to both
herself, but more importantly, her family.

"Right, you can go on the box office tonight with
Kelly. She'll show you what to do. We don't usually
get much trouble, but there is two door staff on
tonight so it should be alright for your first night. Be
down for about eight and you'll probably be finished
for about three." Her boss said.
"Yeh, sure, can't wait, should be a good night." She
replied.

It wasn't how she envisaged her twentieth birthday
to be and as she heard the music of the nightclub
she was working in, she couldn't stop her eyes
filling up.
"You alright love?" Kelly asked.
"Oh. Yeh, I'm fine, I've just got an eyelash in my
eye, that's all." She lied.

SILENT VOICE AND TRANSLATIONS

After a couple of weeks had passed and everything had calmed down at home, she returned. She hated working nights and never intended to do it for long anyway. It was just a way of avoiding the attention at the party.

Her reception was not as rosy though this time, so she buried her head and got back to the driving lessons.

"Helen, phone call for you"
"Who is it?"
"It's Fiona." Said her mother.
Fiona was one of the friends that she had had from school days and still lived in the local town. They shared the same social circle, more or less.

"Hey Fi, you're not gonna believe this but I passed my..." she started.
"Wait, wait Helen, slow down, I've got bad news." said Fiona.
"What, what's wrong, what's happened?"
"It's Jason. Emily's coming back this weekend. He was killed in a car crash last night." She said
"But, I was walking along the beach with him in the summer, he was there, and..."
"I'm sorry; I'll call you when I know more." Said Fiona.

Helens world began to seem like a series of consequences for every time she was happy, or positive about anything. She was soon to get the impression that death seemed to follow her.

Her parents were going on holiday, and due to the fact that the dogs needed someone to look after them during the day when Helen and her brother, Ryan were at work, her grandma came to stay. Since they got the hotel, years ago, she had lived in sheltered accommodation as she didn't really approve of pubs. They now lived in a house near the countryside, so there was no argument.

"No nanna, I can't let you pay forty pounds just for a taxi into town and back." Helen said.

"Well, you say I'm not as good as your other nanna, I'll walk there." said her gran.

"No, nanna, you're not well enough for that, honestly, I never said that, I love you honestly, but it's too much to pay for anyone, not just because of your pension. Let me go for you, yeah?"

"Whatever, ok, fine." She answered.

Helen felt awful now. It was true that she sometimes got frustrated with her grandma, as she was slightly agoraphobic and now she couldn't help but think that she'd probably just denied her a chance of getting out of it.

"Your nanna tells me that you hardly ate a thing when we were away and lived off tinned soup." said her mother.

"What! She asked me to get the soup, here look, it's on her shopping list, I swear!" she argued.

This was true; she could only assume that her nanna had either forgotten or got mixed up as she had never seemed manipulative before. Her mother believed her, because Helen had never had a problem really with food. It was exercise that was her drug of choice.

It was early on the next year that this event was to become another demon in Helens mind.

"Your nanna's in hospital. They think it's her kidneys or cancer." said her mum.
"What? No way, way do you mean or cancer? They must know for Gods sake." She replied.

As they walked round the ward, Helen joined her aunt. She thought that she must have got the wrong bed, as her grandma was unrecognisable. She gasped, and tried to just look at her through the reflection from the mirror opposite. She had lost an awful lot of weight, but looked worse for it. She was grey and resembled a corpse.

In the consultation room, Helen approached the doctor directly.
"Look, I want a yes or no answer. Is she going to die?" she asked.
"I can't tell you that, your nanna is a very ill woman." Was all the doctor would say?

Over the next seven weeks, she slowly watched her deteriorate. Her grandma was accused of having an eating disorder, as she would not eat.
One night, her and her father went to visit, only to find a two day old newspaper and a cold cup of tea sat metres away from her. She couldn't keep anything down, so didn't eat due to the embarrassment of having to be cleaned up by the

brutal nursing staff. Helen thought back to her other grandma and wondered whether the nursing staff at her accommodation had anything to do with her death as well.

The inevitable happened during the seventh week. Her father took the phone call, but said nothing, just cried. Helen couldn't cry. She had lost the ability to feel any emotion long ago. Instead, she ran again, harder, faster, longer.

As she walked down the aisle of the church, she though to herself,
"What a waste of a life."
Unlike her other grandma, where she was grieving for a great person and great life lost. She now was grieving for a life wasted through agoraphobia and self-punishing routines.
This is where things started to change.

Flicking through channels, Helen stopped at a psychology programme. She had long since lost faith in the health system and 'professionals', but this seemed different. She watched, captivated by a woman giving out structured ways and methods of changing your mentality. This was no guru, but a qualified, trained professional with a lot of experience.

Over the next few months, she started to take in everything that was said on these programmes, and started to read all the columns in the paper she could find on the subject. This was her only chance, really, as she had no need to fear someone on the television, they posed no threat and she didn't have to listen.

She read over and over again in order to somehow believe what she was taking in, as she went through the pages of the paper that described so accurately and thoroughly what she was thinking. The counting, the compulsion to keep on doing it, and they overwhelming sense of failure, when on having carried out the rituals, it made her more compelled to do it again, rather than satisfying anything.

She read how puberty was a vulnerable stage for addictions as the body was at an uncomfortable changing period. She read how certain therapies, could undo the damage done, and you could learn how to think logically and control you thoughts again. This was science though, not Hypnotherapy, not some loony, but a qualified, studied fact.
The woman on the screen didn't look at her patients with disgust, resentment or hate. She seemed quite interested in wanting to give them the techniques that they needed to have a happy, long healthy life.

As the weeks went by, Helen was now twenty two. She opened her own company and took up team sports. She knew that if she was going to be healthily involved in sport, she had to do it with other people, and study it.
She took an open course and learnt about sports psychology and how the body changes and adapts

to sport. She also learnt about nutrition and energy expenditure.

The family began to notice a change in her appearance. She took pride in the way she looked, not in a vain way, but in a self respecting, proud way. She became involved in fundraising events and soon applied for a job away from home.

This time, her friends and family knew that when she went away, she probably wouldn't be coming back, for all the right reasons though.
You see, Helen now knew exactly where she had gone wrong. She had never trusted herself, and had been too quick to label herself.

After many months of reading and watching psychology, she now understood that she had never had a disorder of which she thought. The OCD was real, very real, but the exercise and routines and weight control had all been a part of that, nothing more. Once she filled her mind and her life with many more people, activities, and focuses, she had no need to fill in the gaps with madness anymore.

The story ends here, and who knows where Helen will end up. Wherever it is though, she is now well equipped to solve the Rubix cube that is mental trauma. There are still a lot of things she has to overcome, such as her problem with relationships, but now she knows that there are real, tested methods of changing things. A lack of understanding is not a fault; that is why people study to become doctors. If only this treatment had been available in the clinic.

They say that life is fate, who knows, but if she hadn't have been flicking channels that night, things may be a lot different now.

Introduction

This is not a scientific study or analysis. I do not pretend to be medically qualified and so the pages in this book are entirely of my own experience, findings and opinion.

The names in 'Silent Voice' have all been changed, however this is the only adaptation to the true account, exactly as I have lived it word for word.

I do not believe in autobiographies at such a young age that I am. At 22, I have many years to live and many more experiences to have which may enlighten me to other perspectives. So, you may well be asking, if not scientific and not an autobiography, what is the purpose of this book?

To answer that question I will say this. It has come to my belief that psychologists, therapists and those treating mental illness, do not change their treatments as quickly as new ideas arise. This is largely to do with finances in the NHS, but also of professionalism. We do not have enough mice in Britain, to conduct every possible social or medical experiment, and so there will always be room for new ideas and opinion.

When so many of the great psychologists such as Freud have been questioned in their authenticity, and carry a somewhat bad media light, we have to look elsewhere for answers.

SILENT VOICE AND TRANSLATIONS

That is exactly what I did. Although it took many years to come to the conclusion that therapists, doctors, hypnotherapists, clairvoyants, psychologists and key workers at the end of the day are just people. Therefore, they can never have a greater understanding of ourselves, than we do. Then comes the time to ACT on this and help ourselves.

This book hopefully will help some people to realise their own potential in combating their demons independently and successfully, with logic, reason, and example.

If not, I think it may make an interesting read one Sunday afternoon.

I explain my experience in 'Silent Voice' then in the following pages share with you my opinion, theory and lessons that I have learnt. For what would be the purpose of understanding a lesson, if only to have an empty classroom.

Categorising eating disorders

Among the many things that I have come to realise as a bi-product of the account you have just read is the generalisation that is dangerously prevalent in mental health.

I strongly believe that on diagnosis of eating disorders, the patient should be treated or hospitalised according to their level of disorder.
Relapsed patients and 'first time' patients should not be treated in a similar way. This is because the motivations are different, perspectives are different and the chances of mirroring are high. What I mean by 'mirroring' is that when two patients with the same illness are in the same unit or ward, they can develop competitive habits, and learn from one another with adverse outcomes to their treatment.

Recently a programme was shown documenting the lives of two Anorexic twins. This is obviously not the best comparison, as they were related and already had a strong personal bond, however the example showed us that influences with another sufferer can be strongly engaging.

Pre-contemplation, contemplation, action and relapse stages are all very different. The cause should be investigated from day of admittance, not halfway through treatment.

Again, I will use the documentary of the twin sisters to help me with my next point.

SILENT VOICE AND TRANSLATIONS

The reason I think that sub-categories should be established is because it is apparent that OCD plays a strong role in eating disorders with a great majority of patients so therefore should not be dismissed as another illness, but the cause or effect of it.

I had OCD before I developed Anorexia Nervosa, and if I could do, I would have wiped 'Anorexia Nervosa' out of the dictionary and replaced it with 'OCD-affected eating habits' or 'OCD-controlled weight'. I strongly believe that if I had not have had obsessive, compulsive habits, the illness would never have got as far as it did.

I am not alone in this though and have seen many friends go down the same road, all recognising OCD in their disordered weight control.
When watching the twin sisters, you can clearly see them eating and often eating high sugar and high fat products. Therefore you could argue that if they wanted to lose weight to an emaciated state, then how can they 'allow' themselves to do so. Why not just starve? Well, here is where OCD comes in. Everything that they ate had to be monitored by themselves; Calorie for calorie, exactly the same every day; whether it be a crisp, a carrot, or a chocolate bar.

I did exactly the same for six years. I did not starve once the weight was lost; in fact to the contrary I had six meals a day. These meals however had to be at exactly the same time every day by the second. They were weighed, counted and eaten slowly. Then I exercised the calories away. I did not lose weight, but I made sure that the scales were exactly the same for six years, the last digital point on the scales.

This is why I do not believe that I was Anorexic. I was always aware of my body and size. I never thought I was fat. I was ruled by OCD.

So if this happened to me, how many other people have been labelled Anorexic, but actually been stuck in an obsessive rut, and, more to the point, how many years have been wasted before they realised what was actually the problem?

If there was a series of divisions for anorexia or bulimia nervosa which highlighted any indication of OCD, then I believe relapse would be reduced.

Psychology on TV

I feel slightly against the use of TV psychologists. Well, not against, just aware of the cons as well as the pros if you like.

Do not misunderstand me, certain programmes have certainly helped to ease the stigma in mental health, and to that I will be eternally grateful. Also, if it were not for certain programmes, I doubt I would have started to discover or trust any psychological aspects of my own behaviour.

This is because they tend to give a false impression that patients have the undivided, regular attention of a clinically trained psychologist. I do not believe this to be true in the health system today, and I am speaking, again from my own experience, which may of course differ to someone else's.

Hospitalised in 2002, I, and friends of mine, amongst other published authors have all experienced the lack of professional intervention during treatment. The care is 99% through A and B grade nursing staff and key workers with no depth of understanding that is required. One key worker was at school the same time as I was and had only had 2 years study. This made it extremely difficult to either trust, or believe what she was saying, or to respect her advice.

I saw a clinical psychologist once for ten minutes, during MONTHS of treatment. He gave me no feedback, only explained a theory to me that had no relevance to my situation, thoughts, or motivations. I actually told him that when I was in full health gain, I could assure him that my mentality would be exactly the same as on arrival to the clinic. This turned out to be true. My mentality, as like so many other patients was exactly the same. My weight may have changed, however nothing else had. For me, any chemical imbalances in the brain as an effect of the initial starvation were certainly not a cause for prolonged illness.

I find it ridiculous that a TV production company can fund such successful therapy, yet the National Health Service cannot.

Heather Robinson

Without wanting to sound biased, the new generation of 'celebrity-doctors' seem to prefer the use of opinion rather than practise and proven theory. If not prefer, they certainly include it in some of their work. Which is fair enough, but does it have a place either on TV or in a newspaper/magazine article that is intended to be broadly used by a whole spectrum of people? I am writing this book, not as a doctor, but as a person. If I were qualified, I would simply leave opinion out of it, as this could be misleading to a specific case and of course be irrelevant to many.

The danger is when doctors with a high media profile, drift into other aspects of TV. There is a potential to promote their own self-marketing which is completely useless in a therapeutic sense. Of course it may well add to the anxiety of the next patient walking through the door.

I do not believe that you can explore other avenues on TV, at the same time as being expected to be a respected doctor. A familiar face can be a useful tool in lowering stigma and creating awareness of mental health problems. However, if that face then went on to judge and humiliate through TV, press, or public appearance, it is a face wasted and probably adds to the stigma and ridicule in the long run.

SILENT VOICE AND TRANSLATIONS

Explaining mental health problems - The Kite

In trying to explain my problems to my friends or family, I always use this comparison.

If you put a kite away after use, it usually becomes tangled over time. By the next year, it needs hours spent undoing the knots before being ready for use again. Usually a new one is bought instead.

Unfortunately we cannot buy new brains and so as each knot occurs, we need to sort it out before too many more knots cause a complete tangle. When a mental illness is developed, it is an extreme collection of knots. We then have to diagnose each knot via the patient, to undo the tangles and let the kite fly again. One knot is an 'issue', two knots is a 'problem' and a tangle is a 'mental illness'.

Relapse

If we undo all the knots, but it then becomes tangled immediately, there could be a different problem, such as a cut in the strings, or a twig caught in the strings. As a bicycle never work if the tyre is punctured, despite pumping up the tyre. You can increase someone's weight, but if the cause was not body image, but OCD, you will never reach recovery long term.

Figuring out OCD

To simplify my theory, imagine you have been very busy, using your brain all week. Then, at the weekend you stop.

If you stop for long enough, I think that your brain 'makes up' its own dialogue based on all your past thoughts but in the wrong order.

Imagine you are carrying a plastic bag around and every time you think, that thought goes into the bag as a memory.

After a while, the memory bag will have become jumbled up, through carrying it everywhere, so when you have a space to fill in your head through boredom, you turn to the bag for 'random selection' or, OCD.

Unfortunately, there is no easy way to conquer it. The steps are simple but the process in practice is hard. Literally, you stop. Say no. Do not carry out the ritual. Eventually it will become easier as you learn to distract yourself from the compulsion. Initially though, it is far easier to carry out the illogical act, that contemplate having to think about it all day. I can assure you that by carrying it out, or 'giving in' to it, it will not go away, but become stronger. Just like, I suppose if you were to stop taking milk in your tea. If you did it for long enough, it would become a way of life and happen automatically.

I learned how to fight OCD, not by a professional, but by falling asleep and forgetting! The next morning I was actually straining to remember what the ritual was, but I couldn't remember, so I realised that if I said 'no' for long enough then I would forget every illogical ritual in the same way.

I am by no means cured, as I still do get compulsions to count etc... but I say 'no' far more times than I give in., so it does not control my life, or affect the quality of my life. I can hold a conversation without drifting off into thought, and I can leave the house spontaneously without a second thought of A, B, or C.

Who do you want to be?

Quite often I hear of people saying "I went away to find myself" or "I wish I could be like x".

Ask yourself, what you see in those around you that you envy. I do not mean in material possessions, but what aspect of their personality and character do you aspire to. We all at some time have had idols in the way of celebrities, popular people at school, and those in authority.

In my opinion, everyone has the potential of developing their strengths and weaknesses in the same way that those we respect once did. For example, if you admire a champion athlete, trained in the same way and developed the same motivations, you could physically attain the same level achievement as they have done.

In the same way, if you imagine that you are the person that you look up to, and concentrate on the key aspects that you would like to have, such as an approachable manner, or social confidence, you will eventually learn to become like that. It is trial and error. At first you might seem to fall flat on your face. Maybe feeling like you are being ignored, or reluctant to initiate conversation with ease. As with any fear, the only way to change is to ACT.

Once you have done what you have told yourself you cannot do, it becomes easier to do it again and again until it eventually becomes part of your make-up.

I used to think that I could never work for myself, as I did not think any client would take me seriously, being female, young and quite slightly built. Landscaping is quite a physical job, and there are not many women in the business. I swallowed my doubt and anxiety, and once my first job went well; I then liaised with clients as if I had done it all my life. Once you take away the fear, there is nothing that can get in your way.

In the same way, that is how I conquered the motorway. Driving is a good example, as there is no other way to gaining confidence on the road, than getting in a car and driving on your own.

Surprisingly, once I had driven up and down the M1 and back a couple of times, I seemed to become much more confident in other aspects of my life as well. I made decisions far more quickly, and didn't let minor anxieties let me stop doing things.

For me, anxiety is only a problem if you let it become one. We are all built in a way that makes us respond to anxiety in either a flight or fight way.

SILENT VOICE AND TRANSLATIONS

We either recoil and hide, or attack. This is an unfortunate bi-product of evolution, however it does not mean that we are prevented or incapable of doing things, as long as we recognise it for what it is and keep a balanced perspective.

For example, when going for a job interview, we respond to anxiety by sweating, maybe shaking, needing the toilet, feeling nauseous and panicky. We can RESPOND to this in two ways. Either by listening to the nerves by finding any excuse in the world not to attend the interview or maybe keeping holds of the anxiety throughout the interview so that we waffle and come across in a different way than intended. Or, we can see the anxiety for what it is, breath in and out a couple of times, remember that we are perfectly capable of being recruited and see ourselves as an asset to the employer therefore, going in to the interview in a controlled, confident and natural manner. There is nothing that appeals more to an employer than a sense of self-confidence and ability in the candidates own skills.

Even if you again assume that you are merely 'putting on an act', this is NOT an act, but you adapting to the situation with the terminology and body language that it requires.

Again, every healthy human is born with the same potential, but under different circumstances such as wealth, family and situation. This does not mean that we cannot change it though, and those that have realised this have gone on to be either extremely successful or at least very happy people.

True wealth is not apparent in a bank account, however full it may be. It is how you perceive your life to be and how you regard and respect yourself. In my opinion this is what constitutes a happy individual. When you can see mistakes, guilt, regret and misfortune for what they are, and focus on the positive things that you have not only achieved but have all around you from day to day.

The day that you stop asking for approval is the day you reach maturity and self appreciation. This is not easy, and I sometimes find it hard to make a decision without asking lots of people, but the majority of the time I can now rely on my own logic, sense of self and positive outlook to make a choice.

SILENT VOICE AND TRANSLATIONS

MRSA

HOSPITAL BUG-ODE TO TONY BLAIR

You think I don't but I know what you're about,
They go into a ward, and never come out.
Until the end, the reason has no mention,
Stop this crime, I'll pay their pension.

Is it just coincidence they're all post sixty five,
Does that justify your stripping of their lives?
I once asked the doctor, but she passed on a reply,
a government of hatred, deceit and evil lies.

I would not offer judgment; I am an honest man,
But justice is not present, policy a sham.
Where are the priorities to soldiers of the past?
To you I have no loyalty, my family's shrinking fast.

Heather Robinson

CHANGE

Love, hope, humour and soul,
Help keep my mind whole.

Lyrics, imagery, visions and expression,
depicted by a Wiseman can teach us all a lesson.

greenery, scenery, oxygen to air,
things now not so sacred, does anybody care.

one man makes a difference, but more could make
a change,
taking things for granted, while science takes the
blame.

climbing through the rat-race, the problem isn't
mine,
greenhouse gases, time quickly passes, should it
be a crime.

the stock exchange is growing, but progress is still
slowing,
a homeless man tries all he can, but nowhere is he
going.

so I ask you, if only a few can stand up for your
beliefs,
please do it now, one day somehow, we'll end the
suffering and grief.

SILENT VOICE AND TRANSLATIONS

DRAGONFLY

I see things you only dream,
arctic views and ocean scenes,
I hear what you say when they're not there,
every word with me you share.

but alas this is not a love song,
my friend you could not be more wrong.
As I only live a day, oh, why?
Cos I am a mere dragonfly.

Heather Robinson

WHAT IS LOVE?

love in verse, for better for worse,
but what does that mean, as it cannot be seen.
till death do us part, they say at the start,
but is it in haste, or a truth from the heart.

if love is in church, what comes of those outside,
is the purest feeling just kept for groom and bride?
I have not taken vows, but know the depth of pain,
when two souls say goodbye and emptiness
remains.

So what is love, and is it just, for those who nightly
pray
or is it effect of circumstance, around us everyday.

SILENT VOICE AND TRANSLATIONS

SEXISM

if I were a man would you fight me?
if I were lost would you find me?
If I lived in sin, where would you begin?
in leading my path the right way.

The challenge of course, is perception,
a change of inner direction.
for opinion of gender, is brutal or tender,
depending on one's reflection.

So I ask you how you would feel,
if Adam and Eve were real,
when Eve beats Adam, and turns out a badd'en,
would feminine still have appeal?

Heather Robinson

POETRY

Heather Robinson

THE POWER TO COMMUNICATE

I'm trying to communicate,
can't find the words to translate,
never underestimate,
words in any form.

A man can be blind with great insight,
end the struggle and win the fight,
don't give up as one day you might,
smile, and calm the storm.

No one ever told me I'd feel this way,
electric and at peace with life today.
Talk and talk until the message is portrayed,
never underestimate what words can say.

Don't underestimate,
the power to communicate,

don't underestimate,
It's the only way to educate.
A life unlived is one of hate,
Expression, voice and strong debate.

A silent voice is a fallen angel,
Close your eyes and speak to tell.
Lately I've been recognised,
Spoke the truth of a thousand lives.

Long ago I cried with glory,
How things change, I've told a story,
Don't hold back or suppress the pain,
Talking brings you back again.

SILENT VOICE AND TRANSLATIONS

Don't underestimate the power to communicate.

LET ME SPEAK

Locked up in confinement so I can't get to myself,
The only problem now is I can't get to no-one else.
How can I get better with no perspective but my own?
Please come and rescue me I don't wanna be alone.

Let me speak, I'm not empty
Not a child, in my twenties
Trust my voice I won't lie
How do you know if you won't try?

Once you've lost your freedom, creation is suppressed
Believing you're not normal is the hard part to the test
What if someone me I could change my mind for good
Put an ending to the story, break free and be understood

Listen to professionals as dignity they steal,
They might have read and written but they don't know how I feel
You can't define my history with pages of textbook
Your opinion of me, I don't give a ****

TRANSLATIONS

Heather Robinson

RUNNING IN THE RAIN

Starting light which cools my skin.
My clothes now tight that soothe within.
Seeming hydrated, energy inflated,
Faster rhythm the pure has created.

Dripping, soaked, sodden but pure,
Health in my skin much improved I'm sure.
The big smoke is no equal match
to nature's promise of an oasis and fresh catch.

Rain clears the tears which have
built up over the years.
Satisfied, my head is empty,
Running in the rain, do it, be free.

SILENT VOICE AND TRANSLATIONS

PARANOIA

Zombie nation, my creation.
Demons await me at the station.
Eyes are wide, heading my way,
Buzzing, fuzzing, but not hearing what they say.
Turn around, running silent,
tongues are bitter and expressions violent.
Is it the smoke?
Was it the pills?
Speed, weed and even chemical
All left me with very little thrill.
This is now, but do you know what hurts?
Knowing about the greener grass
and not being able to reverse.
2.4 children, mortgage and paid leave;
why am I not in that world?
Why did I deceive?

Heather Robinson

JUST BE

Depth from the earth that's
enlightened by the sky.
No what, how, where or why.
Jeans stained and accounts running dry.
No journey to choose, cause to fight,
guilt, blame or sleepless nights.
Contentment becomes a virtue in the end
with no status, promotion and unnecessary trends.
Practised or preached we have reached the line
where you can just be.
Your eyes have now become mine.

SILENT VOICE AND TRANSLATIONS

AM I WRONG?

A man stopped me as a student looking bleak.
He offered me a job at eight grand a week.
But when I went to work for him I wasn't satisfied.
I couldn't deceive or get sales through lies.

One day my eyes filled up and
I said I'd had enough.
Then I was twenty, now at twenty two
I know just what I want to do.

That man made nothing but cash
and although his car was flash,
I want to make, create, improve and advise.
Am I wrong to want these natural highs?

Simply strumming a song can help a man become
strong.
Grow her a few nice flowers then sit and talk for
hours.
These are my uses of sense, touch, sight and
sound at no expense.
Should I have taken the job all along?
Was he right and am I wrong?

I answered that question by asking what he made.
He told me money was all he made.
I then asked what else his senses created,
with tears in his eyes my doubt was eradicated.

Heather Robinson

WARM TEARS IN COLD RAIN

The clouds have long since broken
But it's the tears that I can still taste.

My only crime to you was failing to hide.
I tried to tell you destination is something deep
inside.
But I can't go on trying to ease your pain
when you couldn't even say my name.
I'm crying warm tears in cold rain.

I'm confused, please tell me why.
It isn't like I'm not use to your lies.
Not a shred of trust remains between us,
only warm tears in cold rain.

I'm nobody's fool, I've had my doubts before.
You could make it right again if only for one more
time.
There was a time when I believed I was never
insane.
Now I'm not so sure.
I'm just crying warm tears in cold rain.

SILENT VOICE AND TRANSLATIONS

FIXED OR MOBILE

I set off to travel but it wasn't long
before a re-occurring feeling came that I was in the
wrong.
Everywhere I looked there were families living right.
Routines set in place morning, noon and night.

I want to see the world and different ways of life,
but I cannot deny the tears
when I see a man hand in hand with his wife.

I will not stop my country hop.
The undeveloped world fascinates me.
The simplest of lives with no complications
makes me question my own motivation.

What do I seek, or want to find?
Why is there so much curiosity going on in my
mind?
Is it the lack of being westernised?
Or is it being ever so slightly compromised
when the once satisfied are shown
a wealth they've never known?

Since my eyes are open to the cruelty of state,
I want to avoid an empty fate.
So if I travelled and paid my way
am I wrong to go looking or should I stay?

Does it make me odd not wanting wealth?
To seek love, write and promote health.
Is the right way the nine to five?
This could easily prove to be a waste of all our

lives.

SILENT VOICE AND TRANSLATIONS

MY RUN

Sweating, pushing and finding a pace.
Dripping and full of anxiety,
this has become my race.
Feet off the ground and going
faster than the speed of sound.
Cheering, but fearing the energy all around.

My dream is to fly harder, faster and stronger.
These encouraging words keep me going longer.
Running through the wall is tough,
can't slow down, but I can't get enough.

Find a rhythm, find a speed,
any which way to take the lead.
The finish is in sight, my posture is tight.
I've cleared my head as the run has put it right
through repression and refuge.

Heather Robinson

[Untitled]

If you were caged in a box for 24 hours,
on release what would you do for the next 72?
Would you run to the sea
now you are able to breathe?
Maybe smile and laugh with strangers,
engaging in dialogue with your arms wide open.
I can't imagine silence on a major scale
where you are forbidden to shout, cry or wail.
Not weeks or months but decades they cower,
whilst under the hand of the corridors of power.
Will the leaders find joy in their final day,
or will God show justice and make them pay?
My youth is still apparent so I cannot answer this.
My culture in comparison allows a life of bliss.
So next time you criticise a man not of our country,
remember how you'd feel if your voice could not run
freely.

SILENT VOICE AND TRANSLATIONS

LND

Clay, bricks, mortar and tar.
Grey, crossings, blocks and cars.
Metal, dust even parallel towers create
chaos beginning from the early hours.

Pavement cracks, a aching back,
possessions carried in tow,
Infrastructure and carbon combustion
produce shortcuts that I now know.

I'm amongst a thousand faces crowding all at once
with different scents drifting in and out.
Just a mile down the clouds are in my view,
pace is lowered, but smiles are way too few.

Newton said people should smile more.
He wasn't far wrong as they scowl instead.
Infusions of wealth, delusional ill health
walk side by side with pride or stealth.

Heather Robinson

WHO WE TOUCH

I don't know my sister and my brother isn't here.
Who can calm the storm and give me warmth
against my greatest fears?
I met him on the tube.
She smiled at me one rainy day.
The remainder of humanity gently leads the way.
You told me tales that shared a truth.
He doesn't know my name.
She'll not forget my face as understanding was the
same.
A passer by looks into my eyes and for a moment
there is silence.
However, thoughts collide and there are faces that
he hides
as if kindness seems so violent.
So geography just separates the burdened from the
free.
Who knows who we touch?
It could be anybody.

SILENT VOICE AND TRANSLATIONS

PERSON X

This verse is written for you,
but in secret.
Your trust I would never abuse.
Your identity is not mine to unfold.
Your confidence I could never misuse.

You know who you are.
I have this message to repay
a kindness you once bestowed on me.
But you misunderstood something
I tried to say.

I admire you without a doubt,
but worry you're wearing yourself out.
That's all, I just care so worries please share.
If I caused offence I was never aware.

My morals and purpose are my priority.
You gave me time when it was scarce.
So now I'm on my feet again I hope we can meet.
Only then will my apology become complete.

Heather Robinson

IT'S OK

I'm just a gym instructor.
They walk in through the door.
Brought here by body, however their minds want
more.
They have the riches and earn a hefty pay,
but just want to hear the words:
'it's ok'.

Some are nervous, embarrassed and cold.
Some are wealthy, some famous and some are
even old.
All are united by the same need as I say:
'Don't worry my friend, it's ok.'

Eye contact is obtained.
In sports I have trained.
But counselling sums it up today,
they just want to hear:
'it's ok'.

I don't know their lives, puzzles,
dreams and daily struggles.
But I can give time and a smile.
I always have the words they crave:
'it's ok'.

SILENT VOICE AND TRANSLATIONS

THE TRUTH ABOUT THE BANKER

I asked him how he was and he looked surprised.
Not accustomed to seeing sincerity in my eyes.
You see success and a mighty career
just influenced a lifetime of tears.
The sadness and pain, waking up
just starts it all over again.
The city becomes a spiritual suicide,
losing faith in those you once chose to confide.

I've seen many places when I
was happy, well and free.
These times were not dependent on financial
prosperity.

They march along near Waterloo,
soldiers in a personal war.
Have they ever stopped to question
what self-promotion is for?

Have you ever made a fiver last all night?
Or spent an hour intrigued at a natural sight?
These things don't cost the world but make it right.
Do you want to help others, or don't you give a
shite?

Heather Robinson

COMMUNITY

Have you ever seen the film *The Beach*?
Was it everything you dreamt of?
Through Bangkok and Fiji into
a hidden land and community.

Out of the system and seeking wisdom,
eco-friendly like the way life intended.
But could it sustain the regret and shame
of leaving others in so much pain.

So instead of running in escape,
go back and rejoin the race.
But instead of taking part,
share the truth inside your heart.

We all imagine a place of free love,
thinking this is what life should be.
But love can be found on your home ground
If we help each other rise above.

SILENT VOICE AND TRANSLATIONS

TRAINERS

They walked with me and ran with me.
Through pain, rain and pleasure they've been with me.
They have been worn down by the more we do.
They are seen by many, but acknowledged by few.

Never far away, we've seen many sights,
gone a thousand miles and scaled many heights.
Always loyal, despite the terrain,
even though I use them again and again.

Had the power and the glory.
They've seen me through the blood, sweat and tears.
I doubt my path but when I look down they are still there.
I wonder where I'll travel with my next pair.

Heather Robinson

FREE SPACE

Just one room that's all I ask.
No material gain do I crave.
A space to paint, write and listen.
Four walls to use the skills that I was given.

Freedom of colour, movement and words,
expressing perceptions of what I heard.
Walls imprinted with journeys far from home;
everything captured in a space of my own.

The real souvenirs cannot be seen,
my memory holds everywhere I've been.
But creative space can never be bought as
the richest of men cannot manufacture thought.

The artist is the person with little to boast.
Their work goes unnoticed as
its not always publicised the most.
Modest is a room with four walls of space.
My wish is to have my own creative place.

SILENT VOICE AND TRANSLATIONS

NATALIE

I've landed where I wanted to go.
I've written about what I wanted to know,
while Natalie sits and waits at home.
She waits for change and waits alone.

The coffee cools to stale,
while the game is set to fail.
Chances are there to take,
but decisions are hers to make.

Natalie hear my voice,
time now to make a choice.
Competence, your turn to choose.
Self-actualisation won't let you lose.

Reflective patterns always send you into reverse.
What's next, will I be chasing your hearse?
Programme to forward and face the front.
It's your book to write so choose your font.

Heather Robinson

GUT FEELING

I remind you don't I?
Do you feel something solid in your throat?
That acid rising from your stomach.
Do you shake a bit and feel colder
because of your truth which I unfolded?

My eyes have levels of vision.
No not superstition, but my mission
to never let other eyes wander like mine.
Confiding and relying was never a crime.

Close those eyes and speak from somewhere else.
If your gut hurts when I'm around then
I'm correct in the clues that I found.
The biggest hint was given away
when I accused and you refused to stay.

What's the danger and where's the fire?
Why so hasty when I still respect and admire you?
Wherever you travel and take yourself,
remember that thought for the sake of your health.

SILENT VOICE AND TRANSLATIONS

PLAIN SAILING

Everything is ok when I take my way.
Follow a map and reason goes astray.
So why is my safety only found when I'm lost?
Can I not be satisfied with plain sailing at no cost?
Drifting, the stream is getting wider.
Open view and more sky,
something is starting to feel wrong.
So I direct the raft to a narrower path,
knowing I'll be in trouble before long.
Everything's fitting in its place,
but this means there's no room or space
for secrets, random acts and risks.
So why do I miss these things?
This is no selfish story
of inner thinking or seeking glory
Quite the contrary, I run in fear
when normal life gets nearer and nearer.
Again this is not in thought,
but experience has taught
that when luck is running high there are always
tragedies, pain and lies waiting around the corner.
You see this is not a human failing,
it's just that life is not always plain sailing.

Heather Robinson

MY CAPITAL: THE CYNIC VS THE OPTIMIST

London's streets are said to be paved with gold,
but they're actually cement grey and cold.
World cuisine, fois gras and warm strudel,
but for me mushy peas and a pack of ten pence
noodles.
Anything goes; you're never a stranger.
But with anyone you're at risk from danger.
Big red buses and a friendly black cab driver,
but returns on the tube are nearly a fiver.
The Christmas lights are all the way down Oxford
Street,
but I've done so much walking that I can't feel my
feet.
Cocktail bars a plenty and the nightlife can blow
your mind,
but where's the enjoyment in over three quid a pint.
Surely it's all worth it for the extra salary?
Not sure about you, but the rush, panic
and emotional explosion must have past me by.
Does all these things cause humanitarian erosion?
Listen my friend; we could be anywhere but here.
The race is irrelevant if your mind is clear.
Yes all this I understand, but wouldn't you
rather be skint amongst the sun, sea and sand?

SILENT VOICE AND TRANSLATIONS

I DAREN'T

I daren't feed the birds as they usually fly away.
I daren't smile at you in case you turn away.
I daren't share the pain as you may see the shame.
I daren't step outside for fear of rain.

I can't speak the truth as you may never forgive me.
I can't stay silent while your health deteriorates so quickly.
I can't climb a mountain just to come back down.
I can't see a future past this small town.

A risk is a goal when defence is high.
A risk is a lover who always makes you cry.
A risk is giving hope to a liability,
but if no one takes a risk you might as well be
a lock with no key.

Heather Robinson

WHAT MONEY CAN BUY

A studio that's mine to design and sing in.
A garden so grand that wildlife floods in.
A pond, pool, vegetable plot, orchard,
king-sized bed and money to go somewhere hot.

Flights around the world with drinks a plenty.
Though money can never fill a space so empty.
Money can not open your eyes to culture.
You have to see in order to change your future.

Can money give you insight or patience?
Can money make an apology accepted?
Can money match eyes so deeply?
Can money replace the rejected?

It cannot return voice to those deceased.
It cannot restore my friend's inner peace.
Humanity, empathy, time and feeling are
the only kinds of wealth that have a meaning.

SILENT VOICE AND TRANSLATIONS

DIVIDED

Found a voice and made a choice,
it was a new history in the making.
Can't keep up or believe my luck
With the chances that I'm now taking.

When visiting home I wouldn't have known
the paradise I left behind.
Now torn between those rarely seen
and those I struggle to find.

Freedom of mind has become a breeze.
I'm not trying to prove anything,
and I'm not trying to please.
But I'm missing one life to improve another.
I feel divided by comfort
with much more to discover.

With cold fresh air I know where I stand.
I'm coping with pressure, chaos and daily demands.
Belonging, knowing easy pace, looking and learning
are all part of joining in the race.

Nostalgia has become irrelevant, it's my world that I crave,
but by being culturally ignorant I do not want to stay.
Whether you are fifty or a thousand miles away
we're always hungry and sated.
Content with a root, but wanting to be more acquainted.

I am the latter, but divided now I stand.
Ecstatic with discovery but sad on the other hand.
What could I be doing in another zone?
Am I right in craving more or should I go back home?

SILENT VOICE AND TRANSLATIONS

JEFF

A girl chatty and smiling gave her time to
an old man who had shining eyes.
He told her his stories, it was a life fully led.
She listened with interest at all he said.

Relatives they became, words given and received.
She decorated his garden on one cold Christmas
Eve.
That year she wrote a card, a greeting of the
season.
She addressed it with love to now a faithful man of
reason.

The gratitude was apparent and he sang to those
around.
Amazing how just a few words could create so
much sound.
The year went by and he grew weak, his fate
becoming inevitable.
She wasn't there to see his now feeble state.

With the funeral now over it was his tales that she
remembered.
Then a sadness became clear when hearing from
his son
that he was buried with the Christmas card she
sent him last year.

RIP XXX

Heather Robinson

PEGGY

My grandparents had all passed.
They had brought me up and I still needed them.
You changed that thought and replaced it
with ways I could always be with them.

You travelled the world, soaked up the sights,
Never stopped talking and livened up the nights.
Always believing, never in doubt
of what life is truly about.

Giving so selflessly and always smiling secretly.
I had you and you had me.
But yet again the best get taken away,
cruelly it happened in a terrible way.

God wouldn't do this, surely not to you.
The more you know, the more you are set to lose.
The more you speak to, the more you have to say
goodbye.
Why create such a soul, only to let it die?

Peggy, I'm not one to say a word untrue.
I promise when it's my turn, I'll be back with you.

SILENT VOICE AND TRANSLATIONS

THANK YOU FOR THOSE EYES

We catch a dream and spread it.
It fills our heads with due credit.
Chances taken, funds forsaken,
a wish fulfilled and success embedded.

The pace is going faster,
but as I slow it down amongst all the chaos,
my mind still becomes lost with
the thought of those eyes I found.

Quite a strange tale of dependence and hope.
Both offended, yet time still found a way to cope.
I became a fish in the ocean.
I apologize if I became a burden
with obvious reaching cries.

When all is achieved and secured
I will reflect how a moment of sincerity,
understanding and integrity,
returned my life from one of neglect.

I talked, wrote and worked,
but never dared to engage with eyes.
A kindness seemingly nothing, but to me much
more
gave me the strength to dispense of all the lies.

You see in all fortunes and pots of gold
there lies a story of how faith
and trust can be restored.
I thank you for those eyes as they're the reason for
now.

Heather Robinson

THE POWER TO COMMUNICATE

I'm trying to communicate,
But I can't find the words to translate.
Never underestimate words in any form.

A man can be blind and have great insight.
End the struggle and win the fight.
Don't give up as one day you might
smile and calm the storm.

No one ever told me I'd feel this way,
electric and at peace with my life today.
Talk until the message is portrayed;
never underestimate what words can say.

Don't underestimate the power
to communicate.
It's the only way to educate.
A life unlived is one of hate.
Use expression, voice and strong debate.

A silent voice is like a fallen angel,
Close your eyes and speak to tell.
Lately I've been recognised because
I spoke the truth of a thousand lives.

Long ago I cried with glory.
How things change, I've told a story.
Don't hold back or suppress the pain,
talking brings you back again.
Don't underestimate the power to communicate.

SILENT VOICE AND TRANSLATIONS

LET ME SPEAK

Locked up in confinement so I can't get to myself,
the only problem now is I can't get to no-one else.
How can I get better with no perspective but my own?
Please come and rescue me, I don't want to be alone.

Let me speak, I'm not empty.
Not a child but in my twenties
Trust my voice it won't lie.
How do you know if you won't try?

Once you've lost your freedom creation becomes suppressed.
Believing you're not normal is the hardest part of the test.
What if someone could change my mind for good;
put an end to the story, break free and be understood

Listen to the professionals as they steal my dignity.
They might have read and written about me,
but they don't know how I feel.
You can't define my history with pages of textbook.
Your opinion of me, I don't give a ****

Let me speak.
Please don't cry.

Heather Robinson

ONLY WHEN YOU'RE PISSED

I have a drink but I'm still the same.
Choosing what I say, control remains.
You are different, warm and closer.
Shame it changes when you're sober.

A night so fake, I was naïve.
You heard my voice I believed.
Was I there to pass the time?
Pissed connections should be a crime.

A nonentity I came to be,
superficial and not in reality.
I went away, it's you're voice I missed.
Shame it's only when you're pissed.

I hope one night you feel alone.
I'm not here I have gone home.
To trust in one, oh how I wished
You liked me sober not just pissed.

SILENT VOICE AND TRANSLATIONS

THANKS

Thank you are words overheard.
The meaning in pictures is better observed.
Sincerity more than I can voice,
giving me closure and giving me a choice.

Unpaid kindness a trait too rare.
Can I believe you actually cared?
Experience teaches you to keep your distance.
I'd prefer to lay down the resistance.

Some are deceitful and never straight.
Others are complicated and full of hate.
So the thank you I give is from someone
whose trust is precious and nearly gone.

Heather Robinson

LEAVING CARE

Family never known,
not a care and no home.
Self-respect is not motivation enough
as finding direction can be tough.

Every corner, page, programme and song
reminds him of how he has none.
Crossing the road was easy to learn,
but the motorway's approaching,
it's now his turn.

Leaving those paid to give a damn,
Christmas and birthdays become a pointless sham.
Don't stare at him and disrespect his voice.
It wasn't his fault,
it wasn't his choice.

SILENT VOICE AND TRANSLATIONS

THAT'S LOVE

When you don't have to see them,
speak, sit or be with them.
Just knowing that you share the same air is
enough.
That's love, that's love.

When you know their sorrow
and admire their smile.
Remembering their voice
and keeping it on file.
That's love, that's love.

Just knowing they know you
is a high that's good enough.
That's love, that's love.

Heather Robinson

[Untitled]

Everyone wants to know me,
But the person I really want to know.
I sense a hint of connection,
but progress is painfully slow.
I do not possess genius or fortune;
my wealth can be measured in mental insight.
As you struggle to express,
I pick up my pen and write.
Am I wrong to be tenacious?
I sense a shadow has been cast.
Communication was more awkward
the last time I saw you.
I'm nobody's fool I assure you.
Obsession is no longer my game.
I'm not asking to explore you,
just that you remember my name.

SILENT VOICE AND TRANSLATIONS

[Untitled]

Paris, London, New York and Milan.
Same places that indulge in the impurity of man.
Kenya, Fiji, Cuba and Peru
bury something deep inside of you.
A different presence and way of living.
Less of an indulgence and more of the giving.
Cleanse the soul, create a whole
without possession is the greatest lesson.
So travel far, keep safe and sane.
Spread your love and then bring it back again.
Fan and Paul stay far from harm,
Then return to build our eco-farm!

Heather Robinson

MYSTERIOUS FRIEND

I'd write you a song but that'd be cheesy.
I'd write you a story but that's too easy.
I'll mimic in verse just to please.
I'll say how I feel but leave out the sleaze.

An accent so mixed I can not compare.
A secret smile and a thoughtful stare.
A mind of memory, which gives no clues
on the struggles and glories that came across you.

A mental level, advanced and shared.
Only the necessary told and secrets spared.
Another time maybe we'll exchange histories,
but for now my friend you remain a mystery.

SILENT VOICE AND TRANSLATIONS

WHERE ARE YOU NOW

What are you doing and are you okay?
Has your mind wandered ?
What did it say?
If it told you lies I'd take away the pain.
I'll embrace you and dry your eyes.

Your book is closed; you won't let me in.
Blurred sense won't dispense the voices within.
I can contradict them; I'll show you how.
Let me look after you and stop this now.

No need for control the mind's better whole.
Where are you now, imprisoned or on parole?
I can break you free and make you see
the peace of mind I found in me.

Do you get a moment of panic and fear?
Where are you now, so close but not here?
Wherever you are believe what I say,
I can fight your war, let me do it today.

Heather Robinson

ITUNES

Stereophonics, electronic and definitely maybe.
Travis, The Fray and The Happy Mondays say
what they see.
Fits the moment, the closest thing to crazy
is when you cry your heart out to music with me?

Emotion a notion translated through song,
justifying reasons why you were wrong.
The Kooks, Kaisers and Radiohead tell
stories remembered in every word said.

You've got my eyes so let's talk.
Morning glory, go out or take a walk.
Ma vie, c'est la vie,
sing a song and say what you see.

Rhythm, trance and beats progressing.
Past regrets that need addressing.
Chill out, mix, have a fix,
all reminders of a first buzz in 1996.

SILENT VOICE AND TRANSLATIONS

DIVERSITY

Sirens, laughter, screams and sadness.
Poverty makes aristocracy seem like madness.
Maida vale, a wealthy creed,
A mile from here someone bleeds.

Tourists, the poor, the affluent and the insane
all living in a city of fame.
Sterling in abundance which means nothing to him.
While Africa is bankrupt, he slowly sips his Pimms.

Those I love I live for.
I would sprint 10 miles and die for.
That's my wealth and nothing more.
The wide eyes of intrigue when with a close friend
and the warm embrace on which I depend.

Status brings contempt when you
have all of what you dreamt.
Bank accounts seem bare
without those you love to share.

Heather Robinson

STRUGGLE

Have you really discovered
the part you thought you'd found?
We'll search for it together,
I'll keep your feet on the ground.

You cannot hide from me, my friend.
I see with similar eyes.
Don't try to fool perception,
to me there's no disguise.

I know the feeling, tell me it so.
I want to hear and I want to know.
No shame in common depth of thought,
I drowned too not so long ago.

You may pretend it doesn't hurt,
but I can see the signs.
There's no point fighting on your own,
your eyes I still recognise.

I see myself behind the smile,
I know that look of doubt.
The day you trust in me,
is the day we'll talk it out.

SILENT VOICE AND TRANSLATIONS

www.ingramcontent.com/pod-product-compliance
Lightning Source LLC
Chambersburg PA
CBHW022200080426
42734CB00006B/512